New Netherland Settlers

Jan Sipken, W.I.C. Soldier, and His Sipken and Sippe Ancestors & Descendants

By Lorine McGinnis Schulze

ISBN: 978-1-987938-27-2

DEDICATION

This book is dedicated to my father Cecil Norman McGinnis.

Without the past we cannot build a future.

Table of Contents

The Sippe or Sipkens Family

Jan Sipkens was a Dutch soldier who settled in New Netherland sometime before October 1674. His marriage intentions were recorded in the New Amsterdam Reformed Dutch Church that month, and they revealed his origins were in Amsterdam Holland. A search of the Amsterdam church records found his baptism in 1656 to parents Sipke (aka Zipke) Auckus and Baefje Jans. The surname in North America eventually became Sippe as well as Sipkens.

A search of available Amsterdam records revealed baptisms of Jan Sipken's siblings and the marriage of his parents. This book details the family in Amsterdam Holland, and New Amsterdam in New Netherland (present day New York).

Family Group Sheet for Zipke Auckes

Husband:		Zipke Auckes
	b:	Abt. 1627 in Workum Friesland Holland
	m:	27 Dec 1653 in Amsterdam Holland
	Father:	
	Mother:	
	Other Spouses:	
Wife:		Baeffein Jans
	b:	1630 in Amsterdam Holland
	Father:	Jan Barentsen
	Mother:	
	Other Spouses:	Coert Eldersen(14 Oct 1651 in Amsterdam Holland)
Children:		
1	Name:	Auckje Sipkens
F	b:	30 Oct 1654 in Amsterdam Holland
	m:	19 Feb 1683 in Amsterdam, Holland
	Spouse:	Teunis Cornelise
	Other Spouses:	
2	Name:	Jan Sipkens
M	b:	20 Sep 1656 in Amsterdam Holland
	m:	04 Oct 1674 in New Amsterdam, New York
	Spouse:	Elsje Borgers aka Burgers
	Other Spouses:	
3	Name:	Evert Sipkens
M	b:	27 Aug 1659 in Amsterdam Holland
	Other Spouses:	
4	Name:	Evert Sipkens
U	b:	06 Mar 1661 in Amsterdam Holland
	Other Spouses:	
5	Name:	Vrouwtje Auckes
F	b:	14 Oct 1663 in Amsterdam Holland
	m:	09 Feb 1697 in Amsterdam Holland
	Spouse:	Tjerck Ottes
	Other Spouses:	
6	Name:	Hendrick Sipkens
M	b:	25 Dec 1665 in Amsterdam Holland
	Other Spouses:	
7	Name:	Evert Sipkens
M	b:	02 Oct 1667 in Amsterdam Holland
	Other Spouses:	

A basic understanding of the patronymic system of naming is needed to follow the lineage so I have included a chapter to assist in that. As well, it is helpful to understand that spelling was not consistent which resulted in many variations of an individual's name. The name variants can be confusing and Dutch nicknames can add to that confusion.

Patronymics

The most common Dutch naming custom was that of patronymics, or identification of an individual based on his/her father's name. For example, Jan Albertszen is named after his father, Albert. Albertszen means son of a man named Albert. The patronymic was formed by adding -se, -sen, -szen and –sz.

The patronymic ending for women was formed by adding –s, or -sdr. Women were sometimes recorded under their husband's name, thus forming a husband-o-nymic of sorts. For example, Maria Goosens (Maria, daughter of a man named Goosen) was sometimes recorded as Maria Jans (Jans being the feminine version of her husband Steven Janszen's patronymic).

An individual could also be known by his place of origin. For example, Cornelis Antoniszen was known in some records as 'van Breuckelen', meaning 'from Breuckelen' (Breuckelen being a town in the Netherlands). The place-origin name could be a nationality, as in the case of Albert Andriessen from Norway, originator of the Bradt and Vanderzee families. He is entered in many records as Albert Andriessen de Noorman, meaning Albert, son of Andries, the Norseman (Norwegian).

An individual might be known by a personal characteristic, for e.g. Vrooman means a wise man; Krom means bent or crippled; De Witt means the white one. Maria Goosens was called Lange Mary (tall Mary) and is found as such in several records of the day. A fascinating example is that of Pieter Adriaenszen (Peter, son of Adriaen) who was given the nickname of Soo Gemackelyck (so easy-going) but was also known as Pieter Van Waggelen/Van Woggelum from his place of origin. His children adopted the surnames Mackelyck and Woglom.

Sometimes an occupation became the surname. For example Smit meant a (black)Smith; Schenck was a cupbearer, Metsalaer was a mason, Cuyper was a barrelmaker.

An individual might be known by many different 'surnames' - and entered in official records under these different names, making the search difficult unless you're aware of the names in use. For e.g. Cornelis Antoniszen mentioned above was known, and written of, under the following names:

Cornelis Antoniszen
Cornelis Teuniszen (Teunis being the diminuitive of Antony)
Cornelis Antoniszen/Teuniszen van Breuckelen

Cornelis Antoniszen/Teuniszen Van Slicht (this is how he signed his name and was likely a hereditary family name based on an old place of origin)
Broer Cornelis (name given him by Mohawks and meaning "Brother Cornelis" in Dutch))

There were also differences over the generations. Albert's sons and daughters took the surname Bradt except for his son Storm, born on the Atlantic Ocean during the family's sailing to the New World. Storm adopted the surname Vanderzee (from the sea) and this is the name his descendants carry.

The Dutch were much slower in adopting surnames as we know them than the English. Patronymics ended, theoretically, some time around 1687 but not everyone followed the new guidelines.

You must also be aware of the diminutives of regular first names, because the patronymic might be formed from the normal name or its diminuitive. For e.g.:

Antonis	Theunis/Teunis
Matthys	Thys/Tice
Harmanus	Harman, Manus
Jacobus	Cobus
Nicolas	Claes
Denys	Nys
Bartolomeus	Bartol, Meese/Meus
Cornelis	Krelis, Kees

Recommended Reading:

Dutch Systems in Family Naming New York-New Jersey by Rosalie Fellows Bailey in Genealogical Publications of the NGS May 1954 No. 12
New Netherland Naming Systems and Customs by Kenn Stryker-Rodda

Zipke Auckus & Baafje Jans in Amsterdam

The marriage of Zipke Auckus and Baafje Jans took place two days after Christmas on 27 December 1653 in Amsterdam [1]

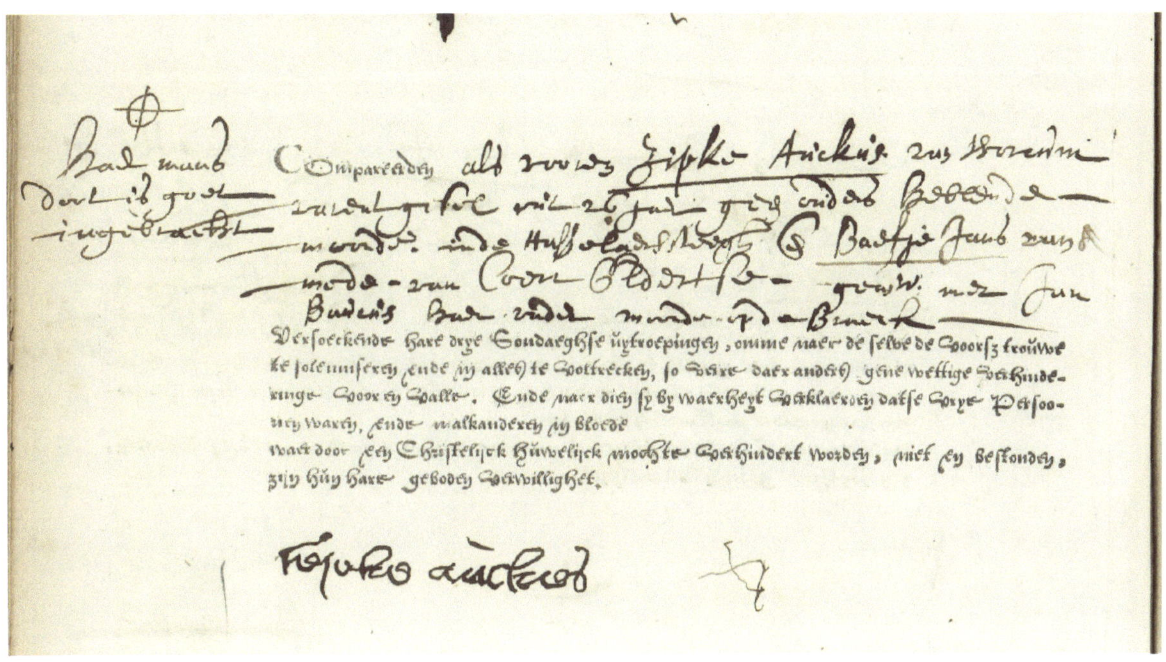

27-12-1653 Groom: Zipke Auckus Bride: Baafje Jans Former husband: Coert Eldertse

Translation of marriage record [2]:
Appeared as before [27 December 1653] Zipke Auckus from Worcum "varentgesel" [sailor] age 26 years, having no parents, living in the Hasselaersteegh and Baefje Jans from A [Amsterdam] widow of Coert Eldertse assisted by Jan Bavens [Badens?] her father living at the Braeck, request their three Sunday proclamations [etc].
[signed]
Sepke Auckes [X]
[margin]
Her man's death submitted [correctly?]
This record shows that Zipke Auckus and Baafje Jans, widow of Coert Eldertse, requested their marriage banns on 27 December 1653. The note in the margin shows that she made arrangements about her late husband's estate. The word "goet" in the original can mean "correctly" or "estate." Such notes in the margin were typical, since the marriage could not take place until she made arrangements with the children of her previous marriage. The presence of this mark suggests she had children with Coert Eldertse but no baptism records have been found in Amsterdam.

Baeffie's first marriage to Coert Eldersen was found in Amsterdam taking place on 14 October 1651 [3]

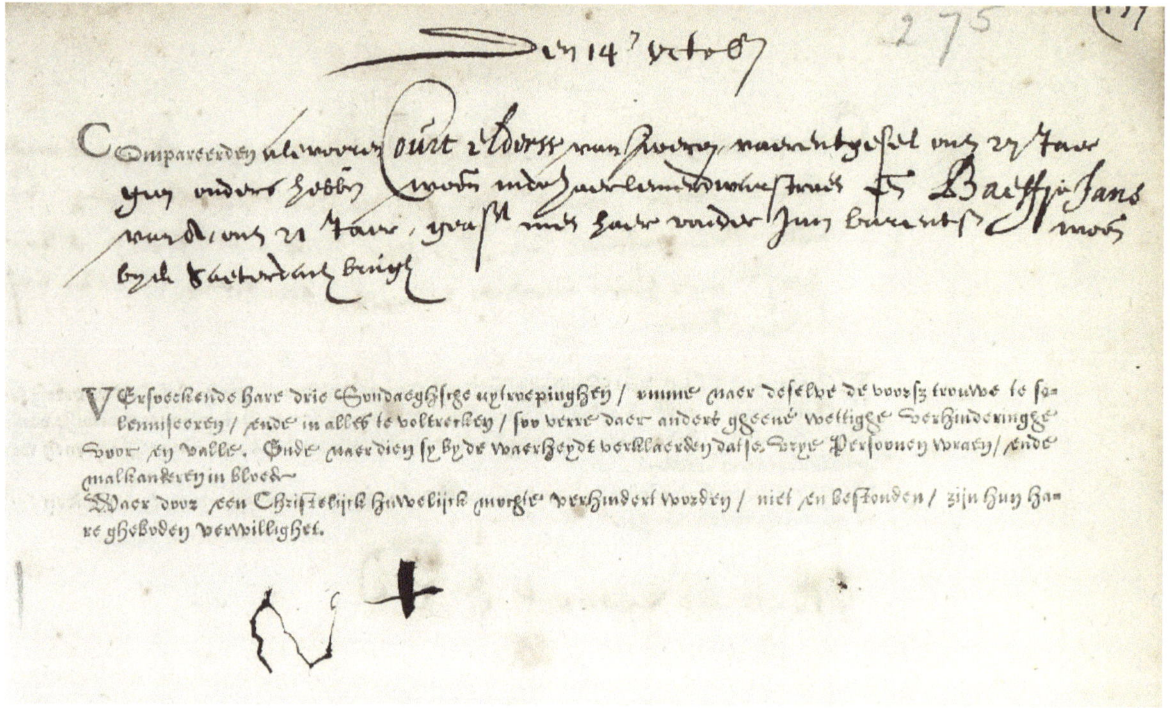

Translation [4]:
Appeared as before [14 October 1651] Court Elderss from Jeveren, "varentgesel" [sailor] age 27 years having no parents living in the Haerlemmerdwarsstraet and Baeffje Jans from A [Amsterdam] age 21 years, assisted by her father Jan Barentsen living at the Saeterdach Brugh, request their three Sunday proclamations [etc] [signed]
[N] [+]
This record shows that Court Elders and Baeffje Jans had their banns published on 14 October 1651. This record shows the father of Baeffje as Jan Barentsen, not Bavens as it appeared in the previous record. Barentsen is a more common name and this name is more easily readable, so this is probably the correct name.

In these two marriages Baeffje is recorded as being from Amsterdam but a search of the Amsterdam church records did not turn up any definitve record of her baptism circa 1630.

Origins of New Netherland

On September 19, 1609, the East India Company ship *Halve Maen (Half Moon)*, commanded by Henry Hudson, an Englishman working for Dutch businessmen who were seeking a passage to the Orient, reached the present-day Albany area.   He had started up the Hudson River just 8 days earlier, on September 11. As the *Half Moon* lay at anchor, Hudson could see an island lying between two rivers to his north. To the west was a vast, unexplored wooded land.

In 1613, four years after Henry Hudson explored the river that now bears his name, a Dutch ship called the *Tiger* left Holland en route for the same waters. Adriaen Block, the captain, was an enterprising Dutchman who had made two earlier visits to these waters. The market for furs in Europe was growing, and Block's earlier visits had convinced him that he could fill his ship with furs which he could sell in the Netherlands as coats and hats.

Two months after he left the Netherlands, Block passed through the narrows that guard the entrance to what is now New York Harbour. Within a few weeks he was anchored at the southern tip of modern-day Manhattan Island, his ship filled with beaver and otter pelts. Unfortunately for Block and his men, the *Tiger* caught fire and burned. Block and his crew were stranded thousands of miles from home. Over the long difficult winter, Block and his men built a new ship, a 44 foot sailing vessel they named the *Restless*.

Cutting down trees and using whatever tools they could salvage from the *Tiger*, the men completed the ship by the spring of 1614 and prepared to sail home. It was on this return voyage that Block and his men discovered Long Island Sound. Block sailed into a freshwater river he named Fresh River (present day Connecticut River) and then dropped anchor at a place he called Hoeck van de Visschers or Point of the Fishers (present day Montauk Point). Having sailed completely around the long island, he claimed it for the Netherlands.

On reaching the Netherlands, Block appeared before government officials. After hearing his story they named the area he had surveyed (from Chesapeake Bay to Cape Cod) *Nieuw Nederlandt* (New Netherland*)*. The name *Nieuw Nederlandt* appeared for the first time on October 11, 1614 in a resolution of the States General of the United Provinces. A charter concerning trading licenses between New France and Virginia was issued to merchants to begin trading, and a settlement was planned for the island where Block had built the *Restless*.

The goal of this newly formed New Netherland Company was to sponsor voyages to the area between 40 and 45 degrees north latitude -- the middle of present-day New Jersey to the coast of Maine. This huge region now had a formal, European name.

It wasn't long before the Dutch started construction on a log fort on an island at the northernmost part of the Hudson River that was navigable for their ships. This was near present-day Albany. At about the same time, merchants in the Netherlands formed a second business entity for the purposes of exploiting their new fur-rich land. This was the Charter of the Dutch West India Company (commonly referred to as the WIC) which was chartered by the States General on 3 June 1621.

The West India Company was designed to stand strong against Spain's interests in the New World. It was empowered to create colonies, settle people, attack Spanish vessels, conduct trade and make treaties with the Indians. The Province of New Netherland fell under the broad monopoly of this company. The capital of New Netherland was to be established on Manhattan Island and called New Amsterdam.

After the 3 June, 1621 Charter of the West India Company, Fort Orange was built. It was built as a redoubt, surrounded by a moat 18 feet wide, mounted with 2 heavy and 11 light cannon, and garrisoned by 10 to 12 men. Around this was clustered a tiny hamlet occupied by the factors and servants of the WIC, who claimed all rights to the entire Indian trade. Although the charter, stated in part that they were to "....*advance the peopling of those fruitful and unsettled parts*", colonization was not encouraged.

The first interest of the Dutch in the Netherlands was the fur trade. Thus the New World represented a business opportunity. By 1624 Dutch traders were establishing the fort near Albany. English colonists were in Virginia and Plymouth, and England was claiming the northeastern Atlantic Coast. Both the English and the Dutch laid claim to Long Island, where the Dutch took hold of the western end, and later, the English settled on the eastern end.

To bolster their own land claims, the Dutch began to establish more settlements. They sent groups of Walloons (French-speaking refugees from Belgium) to New Netherland. The first group of Walloons arrived on *Niew Nederlandt* in 1624 when approximately 30 families arrived. By 1626, these groups had a stronghold on Manhattan Island.

Peter Minuit arrived in New Netherland aboard the *See Meeuw* on May 4, 1626 to become Director of the Colony. He purchased Manhattan from the local

Indians for 60 guilders' worth of trade goods. He ordered that the settlement should be located on the southern portion of Manhattan Island.

The Schaghen letter is the earliest reference to this this purchase. Peter Schaghen, the author, was the representative of the States General in the Assembly of the Nineteen of the West India Company. In the late summer of 1626 he reported the arrival of the ship *Wapen van Amsterdam* (Arms of Amsterdam) from New Netherland. In his report to the directors of the West India Company he announced the purchase of Manhattan Island for the value of 60 guilders. The original of this document is held by the Rijksarchief in The Hague. A copy of the document along with the English translation follows:

Rcvd. 7 November 1626

High and Mighty Lords,
Yesterday the ship the Arms of Amsterdam arrived here. It sailed from New Netherland out of the River Mauritius on the 23d of September. They report that our people are in good spirit and live in peace. The women also have borne some children there. They have purchased the Island Manhattes from the Indians for the value of 60 guilders. It is 11,000 morgens in size [about 22,000 acres]. They had all their grain sowed by the middle of May, and reaped by the middle of August They sent samples of these summer grains: wheat, rye, barley, oats, buckwheat, canary seed, beans and flax. The cargo of the aforesaid ship is:
7246 Beaver skins
178½ Otter skins
675 Otter skins
48 Mink skins
36 Lynx skins
33 Minks
34 Weasel skins

Many oak timbers and nut wood. Herewith, High and Mighty Lords, be commended to the mercy of the Almighty,

Your High and Mightinesses' obedient, P.Schaghen

Courtesy of New Netherland Project, New York State Library

Soon a tiny community was built on the southern tip of Manhattan Island and called New Amsterdam by the Dutch. It was walled off to the north by a thick forest laced with Indian trails. Trees were cut down and small houses were erected. Dirt cart paths became streets. Windmills for making flour were built at the tops of creeks; sailing vessels lined new docksides. To the east, across what is today's East River, lay Long Island.

There was too much to be gained financially by not allowing further colonization. Eventually the Directors in Amsterdam were forced to find a remedy. On the 7th of June 1629, under the title of *Freedoms and Exemptions*, Patroons, those individuals authorized to establish plantations in Dutch New Netherland, were given freedom to bring colonists to New Netherland. Anyone who shipped 50 colonists to the New World at his own expense could buy land along the Hudson River. This man, called a Patroon, had complete jurisdiction and full trade privileges (excluding furs) in perpetuity for himself and his heirs. Thus a type of feudal system was begun in the New World.

The Directors in Holland rushed to avail themselves of the privileges; for the Charter offered them profit and gratification. WIC officials mainly wanted to make a fast profit and return home. They had the monopoly on the fur trade; so the Patroons had a slower rate of return from their initial investment, as well as losses from shipwrecks and Indian raids. By 1635 four of the five original Patroonships had failed, with the only remaining (and successful) one being Rensselaerswyck, run by Kiliaen van Rensselaer from the Netherlands.

The failure of the West India Company and the Patroons to fulfill the requirements of their charter with respect to colonization and encouragement of agriculture was so great that in 1638 the States-General was called on. The Directors were forced to proclaim free trade (including the all-important fur trade) and free lands to private persons under certain restrictions. This had the happy effect of stimulating immigration to New Netherland from the Netherlands. Willem Kieft arrived on board *De Haring* on March 28, 1638 to assume the directorship of New Netherland. One year later an enumeration of buildings erected for the West India Company on the Island of Manhattan, at Pavonia, The Bay, and Forts Orange, Nassau and Hope was completed.

Kieft's tenure from 1638 to 1647 was ruinous. As an administrator he was incompetent, and he did not accept any opposition.

By 1643 Kieft, in his lust for more land, had managed single-handedly to start a large-scale war, named the Kieft War. In 1643 war broke out across Manhattan and western Long Island that resulted in more than 1,000 Indian deaths, including a massacre in what is today Massapequa. Although several of

Kieft's Officers objected to the plan to attack the starving and destitute refugees who had fled from their Mohawk enemies, Kieft insisted and on 23 February 1643 his men attacked with the resulting massacre leaving over 100 Indians dead. The results on the inhabitants of New Netherland was devastating as the remaining Indians quickly retaliated. Willem Kieft, recalled in disgrace to the Netherlands, was lost at sea on board the ill-fated *Princess* on his return trip in 1647. The Princess, carrying approximately 100 passengers, including Kieft, his next in command Cornelis Melyn, one of Kieft's most vocal opponents Domine Everardus Bogardus, and others, floundered off the coast of Wales and sank. Fewer than 20 men were saved; the rest, including Kieft and Bogardus, perished.

Of the earliest settlers, more than half were French speaking Walloons from what is now Belgium. Father Joque, a Jesuit missionary from New France (present day Quebec province) who was visiting the village in 1644 noted only ten thatched cottages. He also reported that there were four hundred people in New Amsterdam and 18 different languages.

Father Jogue wrote to his supervisors in France:

New Netherlands in 1644

By Rev. Isaac Jogues, S.J.

New Holland which the Dutch call in Latin Novum Belgium, in their own language Nieuw Nederland, that is to say, New Low Countries, is situated between Virginia and New England. The mouth of the river called by some Nassau river or the great North river (to distinguish it from another which they call the South river) and which in some maps that I have recently seen is also called, I think, River Maurice, is at 40°30'. Its channel is deep, for the largest ships that ascend to Manhattes Island, which is seven leagues in circuit, and on which there is a fort to serve as the commencement of a town to be built there and to be called New Amsterdam.

This fort which is at the point of the island about five or six leagues from the mouth, is called Fort Amsterdam; it has four regular bastions mounted with several pieces or artillery. All these bastions and the curtains were in 1643 but ramparts of earth, most of which had crumbled away, so that the fort could be entered on all sides. There were no ditches. There were sixty soldiers to garrison the said fort and anotherwhich they had built still further up against the incursions of the savages their enemies. They were beginning to face the gates and bastions with stone. Within this fort stood a pretty large church built of stone; the house of the Governor, whom they called Director General, quite neatly built of brick, the storehouses and barracks.

On this island of Manhate and in its environs there may well be four or five hundred men of different sects and nations; the Director General told me that there were persons there of eighteen different languages; they are scattered here and there on the river, above and below as the beauty and convenience of the spot invited each to settle, some mechanics however who ply their trades are ranged under the fort; all the others were exposed to the incursions of the natives, who in the year 1643, while I was there actually killed some two score Hollanders and burnt many houses and barns full of wheat.

The river, which is very straight and runs due north and south, is at least a league broad before the fort. Ships lie at anchor in a bay which forms the other side of the island and can be defended from the fort.

Shortly before I arrived there three large vessels of 300 tons each had come to load wheat; two had found cargoes, the third could not be loaded because the savages had burnt a part of their grain. These ships came from the West Indies where the West India Company usually keeps up seventeen ships of war.

No religion is publicly exercised but the Calvinist, and orders are to admit none but Calvinists, but this is not observed, for there are, besides Calvinists, in the Colony Catholics, English Puritans, Lutherans, Anabaptists, here called Muistes &c.

When any one comes to settle in the country, they lend him horses, cows &c, they give him provisions, all which he repays as soon as he is at ease, and as to the land he pays in to the West India Company after ten years the tenth of the produce which he reaps.

This country is bounded on the New England side by a river they call the Fresche river, which serves as a boundary between them and the English. The English however come very near to them, preferring to hold lands under the Dutch who ask nothing from them rather than to be dependant on English Lords who exact rents and would fain be absolute. On the other side southward towards Virginia, its limits are the river which they call the South river on which there is also a Dutch settlement, but the Swedes have at its mouth another extremely well provided with men and cannon. It is believed that these Swedes are maintained by some merchants of Amsterdam, who are not satisfied that the West India Company should alone enjoy all the commerce of these parts. It is near this river that a gold mine is reported to have been found.

See in the work of the Sieur de Laet of Antwerp the table and article on New Belgium as he sometimes calls it or the map; Nova Anglia, Novu Belgium et Virginia.

It is about fifty years since the Hollanders came to these parts. The fort was begun in the year 1615: they began to settle about twenty years ago and there is already some little commerce with Virginia and New England.

The first comers found lands fit for use, formerly cleared by the savages who previously had fields here. Those who came later have cleared in the woods, which are mostly of oak. The soil is good. Deer hunting is abundant in the fall. There are some houses built of stone; they make lime of oyster shells, great heaps of which are found here made formerly by the savages, who subsisted in part by this fishery.

The climate is very mild. Lying at 40 2/3 degrees; there are many European fruits, as apples, pears, cherries. I reached there in October, and found even then a considerable quantity of peaches.

Ascending the river to the 43d degree you find the second Dutch settlement, which the flux and reflux reaches but does not pass. Ships of a hundred and a hundred and twenty tons can ascend to it. There are two things in this settlement, which is called Renselaerswick, as if to say the colony of Renselaer, who is a rich Amsterdam merchant: 1st a wretched little fort called Ft Orange, built of logs with four or five pieces of cannon of Breteuil and as many swivels. This has been reserved and is maintained by the West Indis Company. This fort was formerly on an island in the river, it is now on the main land towards the Hiroquois, a little above the said island. 2ndly, a colonie sent here by this Renselaer, who is the Patroon. This colonie is composed of about a hundred persons, who resident in some 25 or 30 houses, built along the river, as each one found it most convenient. In the principal house resides the Patroon's agent, the minister has his apart, in which service is performed. There is also a kind of bailiff here whom they call Seneschal, who administers justice. All their houses are merely of boards and thatched. As yet there is no mason work, except in the chimneys. The forests furnishing many large pines, they make boards by means of their mills which they have for the purpose.

They found some pieces of ground all ready, which the savages had formerly prepared and in which they sow wheat and oats for beer and for their horses, of which they have a great stock. There is little land fit for tillage, being crowded by hills which are bad soil. This obliges them to be separated the one from the other, and they occupy already two or three leagues of country.

Trade is free to all, this gives the Indians all things cheap, each of the Hollanders outbidding his neighbor and being satisfied provided he can gain some little profit.

This settlement is not more than twenty leagues from the Agniehronons, who can be reached either by land or by water, as the river on which the Iroquois lie falls into that which passes by the Dutch; but there are many shallow rapids and a fall of a short half league where the canoe has to be carried.

There are many nations between the two Dutch settlements, which are about thirty German leagues apart, that is about 50 or 60 French leagues. The Loups, whom the Iroquois call Agotzogenens, are the nearest to Renselaerwick and Ft Orange. War breaking out some years ago between the Iroquois and the Loups, the Dutch joined the latter against the former, but four having been taken and burnt they made peace. Some nations near the sea having murdered some Hollanders of the most distant settlement, the Hollanders killed 150 Indians, men, women and children; the latter having killed at divers intervals 40 Dutchmen, burnt several houses and committed ravages, estimated at the time that I was there at 200,000 liv. (two hundred thousand livres) troops were raised in New England, and in the beginning of winter the grass being low and some snow on the ground they pursued them with six hundred men, keeping two hundred always on the move and constantly relieving each other, so that the Indians, pent up in a large island and finding it impossible to escape, on account of the women and children, were cut to pieces to the number of sixteen hundred, women and children included. This obliged the rest of the Indians to make peace, which still continues. This occurred in 1643 and 1644.

Three Rivers in New France,
August 3d, 1646.

On May 11, 1647 Petrus Stuyvesant arrived at Manhattan with the West India Company ships *Groote Gerrit* and *Princess Amalia* to assume his position as Director General of New Netherland. This position included the colonies at Curaçao, Bonaire and Aruba. At the start of Stuyvesant's administration, the population of New Netherland was an estimated 1,000 to 8,000. There is no exact count of the population at that time and only rough estimates can be made. By 1664 it was 10,000.

When he first arrived, Stuyvesant realized that English settlers were spilling into Dutch areas, so in 1650 he negotiated a treaty in Hartford. This treaty drew a line that began near present-day Greenwich, Connecticut, and crossed Long Island, beginning just west of what is now Oyster Bay. West of this line was Dutch, east of it was English.

In the early 1650s, the Dutch and English began fighting in Europe over trade and naval supremacy. This tension spilled over to the New World, where by the mid-1660s the English were trying to oust the Dutch from New Netherland. Locally, there was a desire for more territory and the English were encroaching the Dutch borders.

In 1656 the WIC decided that *"all mechanics and farmers who can prove their ability to earn a living here [New Netherland] shall receive free passage for themselves, their wives, and children"* Colonists were granted as much land as they could cultivate, but without the privileges Patroons had formerly held. The result was an increase in population from an estimated 2,000 in 1648 to 10,000 in 1660. New Netherland changed during this time from a trading post to a colony.

List of Governors or Director-Generals of New Netherland

1624-1625 Cornelis Jacobsen May
1625-1626 Willem Verhulst
1626-1632 Peter Minuit
1632-1633 Sebastian Jansen Krol
1633-1638 Wouter Van Twiller
1638-1647 Willem Kieft
1647-1664 Peter Stuyvesant

Rensselaerswyck Beginnings

Rensselaerswyck was the name given to the large tract of land granted to the wealthy Dutchman and Patroon, Killiaen Van Rensselaer in 1632. It included all the land that surrounded the present-day city of Albany and was situated on both sides of the Hudson River. The colony of Rensselaerswyck and the West India Company officials had long been involved in disputes over jurisdiction of territory around the Fort. When the patroon of Rensselaerswyck claimed all land west of the Hudson River from Beeren Island to Moenemin's Castle (including Fort Orange) had been bought for him. The WIC claimed that the land around the Fort, which had been built six years prior to the patroonship, belonged to the WIC and was not included in the purchase of 1632.

Killiaen Van Rensselaer established a patroonship in the upper Hudson Valley in order to cultivate the land and mine the wilderness for farm and forest products that could be exported to Europe and sold. Before his death in 1643, he hired hundreds of willing pioneers from the Old World and sent them to Rensselaerswyck to be his tenants. These settlers consisted of farmers, artisans, tradesmen, and others who could support the new settlement. Most of Van Rensselaer's tenants settled within a few miles of Fort Orange.

On 10 April 1652, Director General Stuyvesant issued a proclamation. By this proclamation the main settlement of the Colony of Rensselaerswyck was removed from the jurisdiction of the patroon and created as an independent village called Beverwyck. Beverwyck later became Albany. The jurisdiction of the court included Fort Orange, Beverwyck, Schenectady, Kinderhook, Claverack, Coxsackie, Catskill and (until 1661) Esopus (present day Kingston). The Colony of Rensselaerswcyk was not included in this jurisdiction until 1665 when the two courts were ordered to combine.

Rensselaerswyck was the only one of five original Patroonships which was successful.

Early Settlers & Immigration

What we call "passenger lists" were in reality account books of credits and debits for voyages. All such "passenger lists" for travel from The Netherlands to New Netherland between 1654 and 1664 are derived from information on the debit side of the West India Company Account Book. Thus the set of "passenger lists" that we have for the years 1654-1664 are from an account book showing who owed money when they arrived. The published lists draw only from the debit side; the credit side has not been published.

Typical fare for passage was 36 florins for each adult; half that for young children; and nothing for nursing infants. Names were not usually recorded except for the person owing the money. Thus we might see an entry such as "Cornelis Jacobszen van Beest, wife and two children ages 11 and 5" with an amount due beside the entry. The ages of children were given in order to determine the fee for passage.

A typical voyage from the Netherlands to New Netherland took between 7 and 8 weeks.

Many of the early shipping records from the West India Company have not survived, and we must use other records to determine who the early settlers were and when they arrived in the colony. One of these is the 1651 Oath of Fidelity to the Patroon in Rensselaerswyck.

We can also consult the notarial records held in Amsterdam, Netherlands. Approximately 10% of the total notarial records have been indexed, and they hold a wealth of information. Most early settlers to New Netherland entered into a contract with their employer (the Patroon or the WIC or an established settler with money) before leaving for the New World. Many of these contracts can be found in the Amsterdam Notarial Records and include details such as origin of the settler, contract period (2 to 6 years), wages and other agreed-upon details, and sometimes the name of the ship the settler was to sail on. Even if the name of the ship is not given, the date of the contract is usually a good indicator of the sailing date, as the contracts were entered into shortly before the settler sailed. A search of Jaap Jacobs' list of ships sailing from the Netherlands to the New World (and back) can often provide a strong circumstantial case for an individual's being on board a specific ship.

Religion

The established church in the United Netherlands was the Reformed Church. In 1628 the Dutch West India Company sent the Reverend Jonas Michaelius as the first ordained minister to New Netherland. However, even before the arrival of Michaelius, Sebastiaen Jansz Kroll had been sent over in 1624 as a comforter of the sick. Although he began his duties in New Amsterdam, he was soon sent to Fort Orange, arriving there in 1628. The comforters of the sick were required to read prayers every morning and evening, as well as before and after meals, to instruct and comfort the sick, to exhort those who required or requested exhortation, and to read chapters from the Bible and sermons of an ordained minister. The comforters were empowered to baptize and marry, but could not administer Holy Communion. A special form of service was prepared for them to read.

After a few months at Fort Orange, Comforter Krol returned to the Netherlands to obtain a minister for New Netherland. However the settlement was not considered large enough to warrant a minister, and Bastien Krol returned to New Netherland with power to baptize and marry, provided he used the liturgy of the church in his services. When Governor Peter Minuit arrived in 1626 to take charge of the colony, he ordered that the settlement should center about the southern portion of Manhattan Island. Soon after Peter Minuit's order, Comforter Krol left Fort Orange to become the first comforter at New Amsterdam.

In 1632 the *Patroon* Kiliaen van Rensselaer gave instructions that settlers in the Colony of Rensselaerswyck should come together every Sunday and on holidays to read passages and chapters from the Bible. Brant Peele van Niekerck was authorized by van Rensselaer to read from the Bible.

The church founded at Albany in 1640 was the only one north of Esopus with a permanent ministry - other than Schenectady. All babies were baptised and their names entered in the *Doop Boek*, but sadly Albany's records are scanty prior to 1684. Many are lost completely. The population of Fort Orange is not known in this early period, but it was small. The first church built in 1648 was 84x19 feet, and consisted of only nine benches for those attending services. This church was still in use until 1656.

It was not until 1642 that Dominie Johannes Megapolensis was hired to preach in Rensselaerswyck. There was no church building, and it is not known where he held services. In 1649 Dominie Megapolensis was called from

Rensselaerwyck (Albany) to assume charge at Manhattan. For the next year, his son-in-law, Dominie Grasmeer, conducted the Albany area services.

The *Patroon's* trading house on the west side of the Hudson River, had been turned into a church in March 1648. The *dominie* was an ordained minister of the Dutch Reformed Church sent by the church leadership in the Netherlands to minister to the Albany congregation. Dominie Gideon Schaets arrived in the Colony in July 1652 and was minister until his death in 1694. Both *dominies* (ministers) and Deacons (lay leaders) staffed the church. The Deacons were prominent Albany businessmen and officials.

In June 1656 the cornerstone of the new Dutch Reformed Church was laid. There are no known surviving registers from the church at Beverwyck/Albany before 1684.

Albany Dutch Reformed Church.
Courtesy New York State Museum

List of Ministers at the Albany Dutch Reformed Church

Johannes Megapolensis, Jr. 1642-52
Gideon Schaets, 1652-1691
Godefridus Dellius, 1683-1699
Johannes Nucella, 1699-1700
Johannes Lydius, 1700-1710
Petrus Van Driessen, 1712-1738
Cornelis Van Schie, 1733-1744
Theodorus Frielinghuysen,1746-59
Eilardus Westerlo, 1760-1790
John Bassett, 1787-1804
John B. Johnson, 1796-1802

Money & Money Substitutes in New Netherland

Native Indians did not use currency. Instead they collected oblong shells which they polished and cut into beads. The finished highly polished beads were often attached to clothing. They were used as necklaces, belts and frequently strung in rows. These lengths of shells called *wampum* were often given as gifts. All beads were made up of highly polished cylinders about 1/8 " diameter and ¼" long, drilled length-wise and strung on ropes of hemp or the tendons of animals. While the local area dictated what shells could be used, in general black beads came from the local clam, known as the *quahaug*; while white beads came from winkles or periwinkles.

Indian beads were known by a variety of names among the early colonists – wampum, wampom-peage, wampeage, peage (which referred to beads that were strung), and in some localities such as New Netherland, seawan or seawand. In general the Dutch called it *seawan* (which they used for all shelled money), the English wampum. For the Indians, *wampum* referred strictly to white beads. They called their black beads *suckaubock*. The colonists used what they considered the generic term of *wampum* to refer to both varieties.

In 1609 Hudson's men received strings of beads from local Indians. The first European to use these beads for barter was a Dutch fur trader named Jacob Eelckens. In 1622 Eelckens demanded a ransom for a Pequot *sachem* (chief) on Long Island. The *wampum* Eelckens was given brought him more furs in trade than conventional trade goods. Before long the West India Company, recognizing a good thing, had their agents purchase all the *wampum* they could and take it north to Fort Orange. There they used it to buy furs from the Mahicans. Almost overnight *wampum* was functioning like money.

When Dutch traders encountered *wampum* they adopted it as a money substitute. Although more convenient than commodity money several problems developed with the use of *wampum*. It had no intrinsic value, and anyone could collect some shells and produce their own currency. With no central minting operation the quality of these products was often substandard. Shopkeepers needed to keep a vigilant eye for inferior *wampum* but there was no legislation in place that allowed them to refuse poor quality beads. Further, the amount of *wampum* produced was unregulated, and this eventually caused an oversupply.

In New Netherland *wampum* was legislated at four beads to the *stiver*, which was the Dutch equivalent of the English penny. However, so many poor quality unstrung beads were put into circulation that in April 1641 a law was passed prohibiting the use of unpolished beads during the month of May. During that month these poorer beads would be accepted in payment of taxes but only if they were strung and then only at the discounted rate of six beads to the stiver. The problems continued, and in May 1650 an ordinance was passed prohibiting the use of loose *wampum*. This law also further discounted poorly made *wampum* that circulated on string, so that they traded at the rate of eight beads to the stiver. As more and more *wampum* flooded the market the value of all beads declined.

In 1661 Director General Stuyvesant addressed the colonists' concern over the steady inflation of *wampum*. Much of it was "unpierced and half-finished, made of stone, bone, glass, shells, horn, nay even of wood, and broken". Huge quantities of this inferior *wampum* was being dumped in the colony by the English with the result that wages and cost of goods rose. Stuyvesant ordered that all wampum used as money must first be strung, and its value was fixed at six white or 3 black beads per *stiver* for high quality trade *wampum*, and eight white or four black beads per *stiver* for inferior quality.

Seawant, or unstrung beads, which had been prohibited from daily commerce in 1650, was still used for tax payments. As late as 1693 commuters on the New York and Brooklyn ferry could pay with either two pence in silver or eight *stivers* in *wampum*. The last recorded exchange of *wampum* as money was in New York in 1701.

Gen 2: Auckje Sipkens 1654-? & Teunis Cornelise

Auckje was baptised on October 30, 1654 in Westerkerk in Amsterdam to parents Sipke Auckes and Baefje Jans. She does not appear to have left Holland.

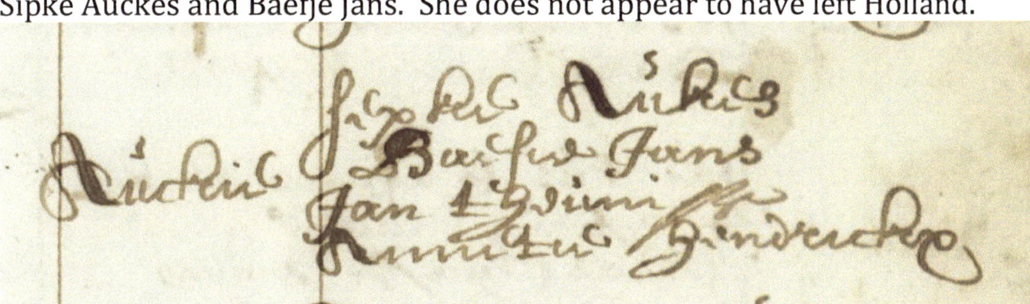

Baptism Auckje - 30-10-1654 [5]

She married Teunis Cornelise on 19 February 1683 in Amsterdam.

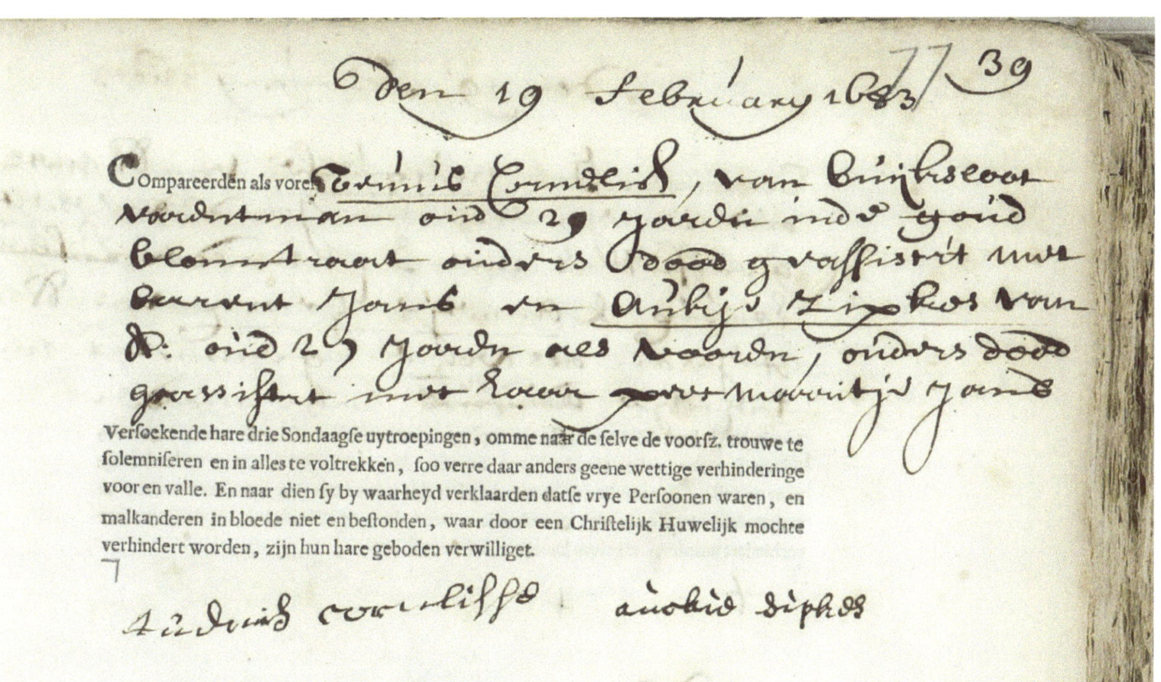

19-02-1683 - Cornelisz, Teunis - Sipkes, Aukje [6]

Children baptised in Amsterdam were:
1. Cornelis, 17-10-1685 in Noorderkerk to Teunes Cornelisz & Auke Sipkes Sp. Grietje Cornelis (possibly Teunis' sister or mother) [7]
2. Cornelis 17-08-1687 in Noorderkerk to Tunes Cornelisz & Auckje Sipkes [8]
3. Grietje 19-01-1689 in Noorderkerk to Tuense Cornelisz & Auke Sipkes Sp. Marritje Sipkens [9]

4. Cornelis 18-01-1693 in Noorderkerk to Tuenes Cornelisse & Auke Sipkes. Sp. Vrouwtje Sipkens [10]

Gen 2: Jan Sipkens 1656-? & Elsje Borgers

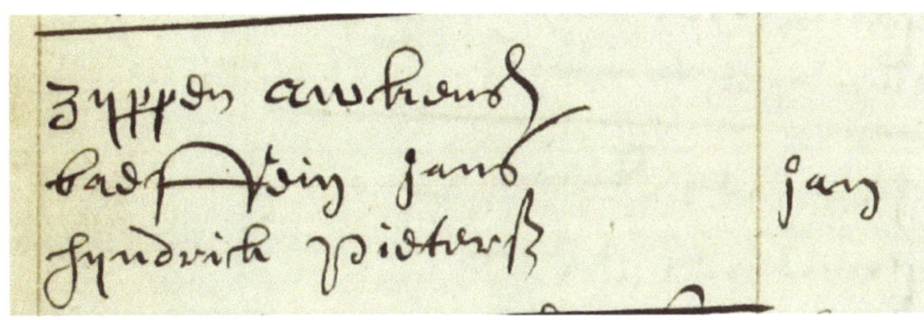

Baptism of Jan - 20-09-1656 [11]

It appears that Jan was the only child of Aucke Sipkes and Baefje Jans who left Holland and settled in New Netherland. We find him marrying in 1674 in New Amsterdam (present-day New York City) Reformed Dutch Church. His marriage intentions are dated 14 October and read:

1674 Eodem [14 Oct]. Jan Sipkens, Soldaet, j. m. Van Amsterd., en Elsje Burgers, j. d. Van N. Orangien. 31 Octob.

Translation: *Jan Sipkens, soldier, unmarried man from Amsterdam, and Elsje Burgers, unmarried woman from New Orange (Albany)* Their intentions were filed on October 14 and they married on October 31.

Elsje was the daughter of Burger Joris and Engeltie Mans. There is mention of Burger Joris[zen]:

"Burger Joris, from Hirschberg, Silesia, was in New Amsterdam in 1637. For some time he worked in the colony of Rensselaerswyck. in 1639 he removed to New Amsterdam where he the same year married Engeltje Mans of Sweden" [12]

The information above is verified by the New Amsterdam marriage record as follows:

1639, 18 Dec; Borger, Joriszen, j.m. Van hersberg, in Silesien [Germany], en Engeltje Mans, j.d. Van Coimxste in Sweden.

Family Group Sheet for Jan Sipkens

Husband:		Jan Sipkens
	b:	20 Sep 1656 in Amsterdam Holland
	m:	04 Oct 1674 in New Amsterdam, New York
	Father:	Zipke Auckes
	Mother:	Baeffein Jans
	Other Spouses:	

Wife:		Elsje Borgers aka Burgers
	b:	Fort Orange (Albany) New York
	Father:	Burger Joriszen
	Mother:	Engeltie Mans
	Other Spouses:	

Children:

1	Name:	Baefken Sipkens
F	b:	18 Aug 1675 in New Amsterdam, New York
	m:	01 Sep 1699 in New York
	Spouse:	Johannes Hendrickse VandeWater
	Other Spouses:	

2	Name:	Engeltie Sipkens
F	b:	04 Aug 1677 in New York
	m:	20 Jul 1700 in New York City, New York
	Spouse:	Thomas Evans
	Other Spouses:	

3	Name:	Burgher Sipkens
M	b:	Abt. 1679 in New York
	m:	1712
	d:	Bef. 19 Mar 1747 in New York
	Spouse:	Maria Hibbon
	Other Spouses:	Rebecca Gerritse Onkelbach(27 Apr 1728 in New York)

4	Name:	Catharina Sipkens
F	b:	12 May 1680 in New York
	Other Spouses:	

5	Name:	Tsipken Sipkens
M	b:	20 Jun 1682 in New York
	Other Spouses:	

6	Name:	Anna Maria Sipkens
F	b:	25 Oct 1684 in New York
	m:	03 Oct 1702 in New York
	Spouse:	Harmen Lutjens
	Other Spouses:	Hendrick Frans(24 Nov 1709 in New York)

7	Name:	Jan Sipkens
M	b:	21 Nov 1686 in New York
	Other Spouses:	

8	Name:	Jan Sipkens
M	b:	10 Jun 1688 in New York
	Other Spouses:	

9	Name:	Joris Sipkens
M	b:	10 Aug 1690 in New York
	Other Spouses:	

10	Name:	Reynier Sipkens
M	b:	17 Nov 1695 in New York
	Other Spouses:	

Husband:		Burgher Sipkens
	b:	Abt. 1679 in New York
	m:	27 Apr 1728 in New York City, New York
	d:	Bef. Oct 1735 in New York
	Father:	Jan Sipkens
	Mother:	Elsje Borgers aka Burgers
	Other Spouses:	Maria Hibbon
Wife:		Rebecca Gerritse Onkelbach
	b:	08 Jan 1693 in New York
	d:	Bet. 11 Oct 1749-07 Dec 1755 in New York
	Father:	Gerrit Adamse Onkelbach
	Mother:	Elizabeth Van Schayck
	Other Spouses:	Johannes Bresteede(Bef. 1713)

Children:

1	Name:	Burger Sipkens
M	b:	28 Sep 1729 in New York City, New York
	Other Spouses:	
2	Name:	Onkelbag Sipkens
M	b:	28 Sep 1729 in New York City, New York
	Other Spouses:	

Husband:		Johannes Bresteede
	m:	Bef. 1713
	d:	Bet. 1722-1728
	Father:	
	Mother:	
	Other Spouses:	
Wife:		Rebecca Gerritse Onkelbach
	b:	08 Jan 1693 in New York
	d:	Bet. 11 Oct 1749-07 Dec 1755 in New York
	Father:	Gerrit Adamse Onkelbach
	Mother:	Elizabeth Van Schayck
	Other Spouses:	Burgher Sipkens

Children:

1	Name:	Elizabeth Bresteede
F	b:	07 Jan 1713 in New York City, New York
	Other Spouses:	
2	Name:	Andries Bresteede
M	b:	20 Mar 1715 in New York City, New York
	Other Spouses:	
3	Name:	Annatje Bresteede
F	b:	25 Jan 1716 in New York City, New York
	Other Spouses:	
4	Name:	Gerardus (Garrett) Bresteede
M	b:	20 Aug 1718 in New York City, New York
	d:	Bef. 19 Mar 1747
	Other Spouses:	
5	Name:	Rebecca Bresteede
F	b:	13 Jun 1722 in New York City, New York
	Other Spouses:	

Gen 2: Evert Sipkens 1659-?

Evert, the son of Sipke Auckes and Baefjie Jans, was baptised in Amsterdam in 1659.

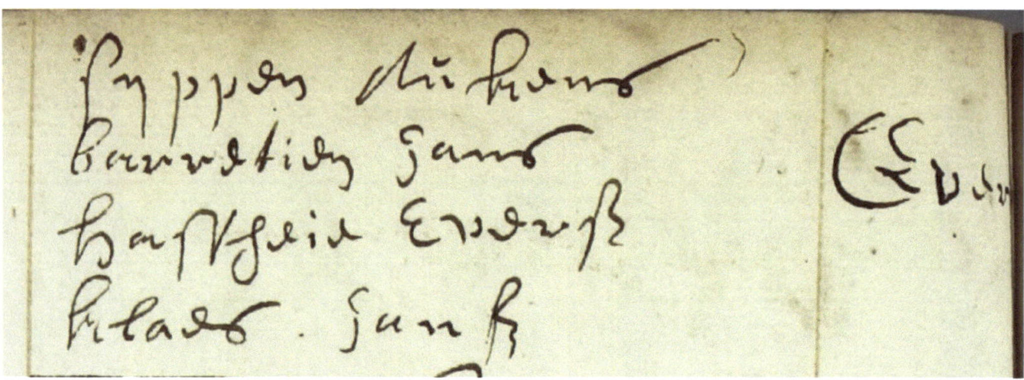

Baptism , Evert - 27-08-1659 [13]

Evert presumably died young sometime before March 8, 1661 at which time another son was born to Sipke and Baefje and named Evert. This baptismal record is a good example of the variant name spellings (and alternate names) of Dutch individuals – here Baefjie has become Barendje.

Gen 2: Evert Sipkens 1661-1666

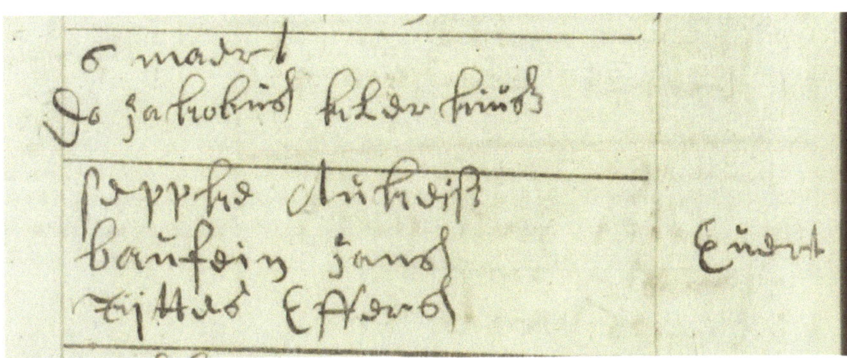

Baptism Evert - 06-03-1661 [14]

This Evert presumably also died young sometime before October 2, 1667 at which time another son was born to Sipke and Baefje and named Evert. The family buried two children (whose names were not given) in Amsterdam on February 14, 1666 and on March 25, 1666. One was almost certainly Evert and the other possibly Hendrick.

Gen 2: Vroutjie Sipkens 1663-1743

Vrouwtje's baptism occurred in the Amsterdam North Church in 1663. Sponsors were Trentjen Jurians and Marrjen Gerrits.

Baptism , Vrouwtje - 14-10-1663 [15]

Vroutjie married Tjerk Ottese on 09 February 1697 in Amsterdam.

09-02-1697 - Ottes, Tjerck - Sipkes, Vroutje [16]

9 February 1697
Appeared Tjerck Ottes from A [Amsterdam] "treckwerker" [pull worker, i.e. someone who pulls loads], age 30, at the Haerlemsedijk assisted by his mother Marritje Doedes and Vroutje Sipkes from A [Amsterdam] age 33 in the Lindestraet parents deceased assisted by her sister Aeltje Sipkes request their three Sunday proclamations [etc]
[signed] [17]

Tjerck Ottes was baptised in the Lutheran Church in Amsterdam on December 13, 1667. His parents were recorded as Otte Tiercks and Maria Doedes.

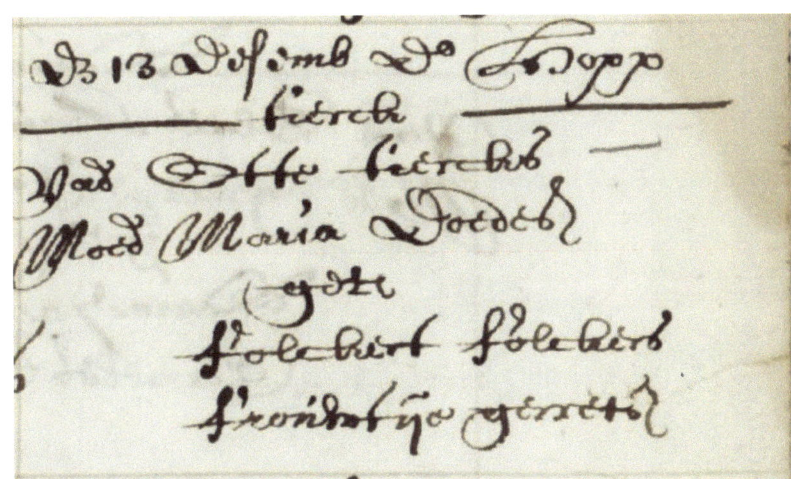

Tierck - 13-12-1667 [18]

The baptisms of three children in Amsterdam were found For Tjerck Ottes and Vroutje Sipkens: Otto in the Westerkerk on 12 April 1697, Sipke in the Lutheran Church on 7 January 1699 and Maritje in the Westerkerk on 11 August 1700.

Vroutjie was buried on 2 September 1734 as the widow of Tjerk Ottesz.

Ottesz, Tjerk - Sipkes, Vroutje - 02-09-1734 [19]

Gen 2: Hendrick Sipkens 1665-?

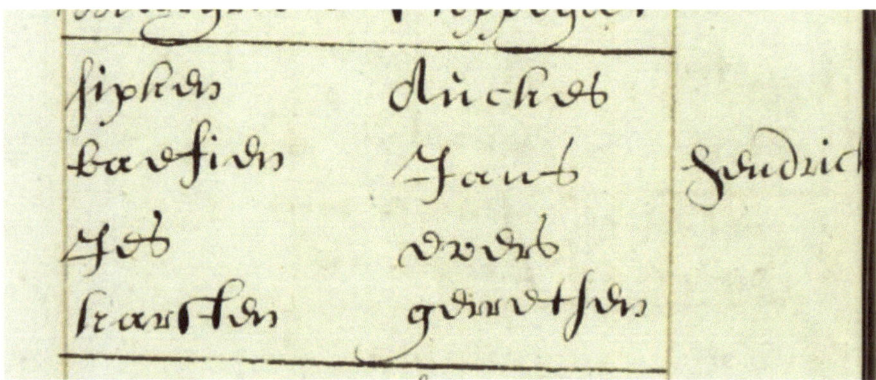

Baptism Hendrick - 25-12-1665 [20]

There is no further record of Hendrick. The family buried two children (whose names were not given) in Amsterdam on February 14, 1666 and on March 25, 1666. One was possibly Hendrick.

Gen 2: Evert Sipkens 1667-?

Baptism , Evert - 02-10-1667 [21]

On November 3, 1669 Sipken Auckes buried a child (no name was given) in Amsterdam and Evert could be the child who died.

Gen 3: Baefje Jans Sipken & Johannes Van de Water

Johannes van de Water was baptised in New Amsterdam, New Netherland on
February 19, 1673 to Hendrick Vande Water and Margrietje (Grietie) Vermeulen
The witnesses were Cornelis Pluvier and Sara Webbers. Johannes died presumably
August 28, 1731

Johannes and Baefje were married in New York on September 1, 1692. The church
record records the couple as: *Johannes Van de Water, j.m., Van N. Yorck, en Baefie Jans,
j.d., als boven, beyde wonende alheir. den 1 Sept.*

*Translation: Johannes Van de Water, unmarried man from New York, and Baefie Jans,
single woman, as above, both living near here, on 1 September*

Children's baptisms in New Amsterdam were:

1. 1692 23 Nov; Johannes V. Water, Baefje Jans; **Hendrick**; Jan Sipkens, Grietje
   Van de Water
2. 1695 22 May; Johannes Van de Water, Baefje Jans Sipps; **Elsje**; Manus Borger,
   Elsje Borger
3. 1697 Jun 20; Johannis Van de Water, Baefje Jans; **Jan**; Theunis Tibout,
   Ariaantje Bennet
4. 1700 10 Mar; Johannis Van de Water, Baefje Sipkens; **Margarita**; Balthazar
   Bayard, Maria Van der Water wife of Theunis Tibout
5. 1702 26 Apr; Johannes Van de Water, Baefje Sipkens; **Elsie**; Johannes
   Pouwelse, Elizabeth Van de Water
6. 1704 24 May; Johannis Van de Water, Baafje Sipkens; **Johanna**; Harme
   Luykasse, Anna Maritie Sipkens
7. 1705 23 Sept; Johannis Van de Water, Baefje Sipke; **Engeltje**; Willem Van de
   Water & wife Aegje Ringo
8. 1707 14 Sept; Johannes Van de Water, Baafje Sippe; **Albartus**; Willem
   Bennet, Pieternella Kloppers
9. 1710 9 Jul; Johannes Van de Water, Baefje Sippe; **Ariaantje**; Burger Sippe,
   Anna Maria Sippe

Gen 3: Engeltie Sipkens & Thomas Evans

Engeltie was baptised 4 August 1677 in New Amsterdam. Her baptismal record reads "Jan Sipkens, Elsje Borgers - Engeltie. [sponsors] David Hendrickszen, Anna Borgers"

Her marriage to Thomas Evans from London England took place in the same church on 20 July 1700. The church record reads " 1700 den 20 dicto [July]. Thomas Evans, Jm. van London in Englt. en Engeltje Siphens, Jd. van N. Yorck. beyde woonende alhier. den 13 dicto." [22]

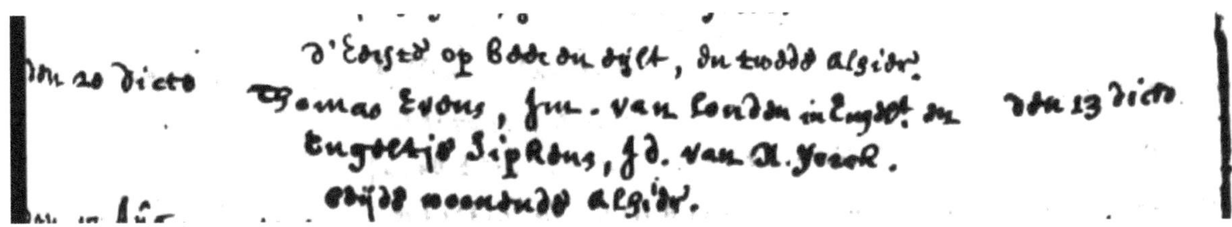

No children have yet been found for this couple.

Gen 3: Anna Maria Sipkens & 1. Harmen Lutjens & 2. Hendrick Frans

The marriage intentions of Harmen Lutjens, young man from Hamburg, and Anna Maria Sipkens, young woman from New York were recorded in the New York church on 3 October 1702 as *den 3 Oct; Harmen Lutjens, j.m. Van Hamb'h, met Anna Maria Sipkins, j.d. Van N. York; [ndg]* [23]

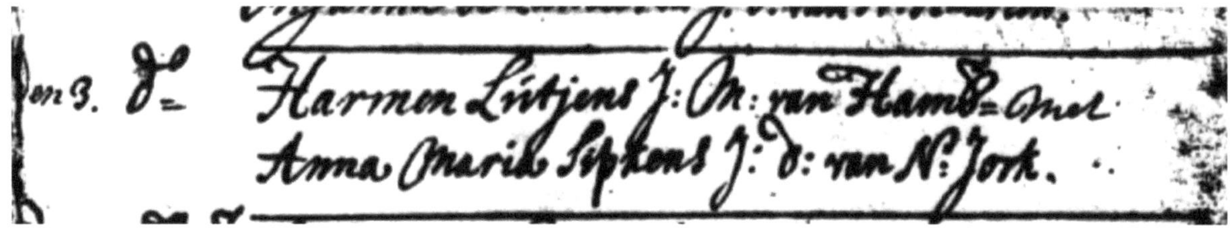

Children with Harmen Lutjens:
1. 1704 27 Dec; Harme Luykasse, Anna Maria Sippe; **Harme**; Johannis Van de Water, Elsie Sippe
2. 1707 2 Jul; Harme Luykasse, Anna Maria Sippe; **Jan**; Johannes Burger & wife Helena

Marriage #2:
1709 do 21; Hendrik Fransse, Wed'r V. N. York, met Anna Maria Sipkens, Wed. V. Harm: Lucasz V. N. York; 24 Nov.

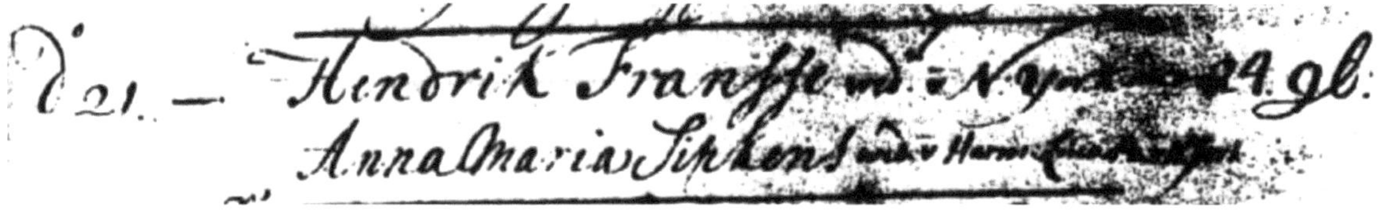

Children with Hendrik Franse:
1. 1711 3 Jun; Hendrik Franse, Anna Maria Sippe; **Anna**; Sjaert Olfertz & wife Dorathe Grienham
2. 1713 20 Sept; Hendrik Franse, Anna Maria Sippe; **Jan**; Johannes Van de Water & wife Baefje
3. 1715 6 Jun; Hendrik Franse, Anna Maria Sipkens; **Hendrikus**; Sjoert Olphertse, Maria Sipkens
4. 1717 1 Sept; Hendrik Franse, Anna Maria Sipkens; **Elsje**; Johannes Van de Water, Maria Leanerd
5. 1719 13 Sept; Hendrik Fransen, Maria Sipkens; **Jan**; Burger Sipkens, Maria France
6. 1721 7 Jun; Hendrik Franse, Anna Maria Sippe; **Elizabeth**; Johannes Van de Water, Margrietjc Kitling

7. 1725 26 Feb; Hendrik Franse, Anna Maria Sippe; **Johannes**; Willem Bant, Geertruy Burgers

Hendrick Frans was born to parents Frans Hendrickszen and Belitje Joris. He was baptized January 12, 1673 at the Reformed Dutch Church in New Amsterdam with his grandfather, Joris Stephenszen, and Jannetje Hendricks as witnesses. The identity of his first wife is not known.

Gen 3: Burger Sipkens & 1. Marytje Hibon & 2. Rebecca Gerritse Onkelbach

Burger Sipkens married twice – the first time to Marytje Hibon. Jan Hibon, who was almost certainly her father, with wife Geertruyd Barents, were early settlers in New Amsterdam. Jan was released as a cadet in the WIC (West India Company) on July 2, 1658. [24]

Jan was living in Brooklyn in 1660 as he was censured by the church that year. By 1669 he was dead as his widow remarried that year to Jan Janszen Poppen. [25]

Marriage of Burger & Marytje 20 June 1712 in New York City

Children from #1:
1. 1713 25 Mar; Burger Sippe, Marytje Hibon; **Geertruy**; Johannes Hibon, Maria Narbury (no doubt named in honour of Marytje's mother)
2. 1714 8 Dec; Burger Sipkens, Maria Hibon; **Elsje**; Johannes Van de Water & wife Baafje Sipkens (named in honour of Burger's mother)
3. 1717 19 May; Burger Sipken, Maria Hibon; **Jan**; Jan Hibon, Debora Sipkens (probably named in honour of Marytje's father but possibly Burger's father)
4. 1719 11 Apr; Burger Sipkens, Maria Hibon; **Burger**; Pieter Hibon, Elizabeth Mansfield
5. 1720 14 Aug; Burger Sippe, Maria Hibon; **Geertruyd**; Pieter Hibon, Maria Narbury
6. 1724 26 Apr; Burger Sippe, Maria Hibon; **Maria**; Pieter Hibon & wife Maria

Burger Sipkens married Rebecca Onkelbag on 27 April 1728 in New York. Rebecca was the daughter of Gerrit Onkelbag who mentioned her in his will dated 1732. At her marriage to Burger, she was the widow of Johannes Brestede.

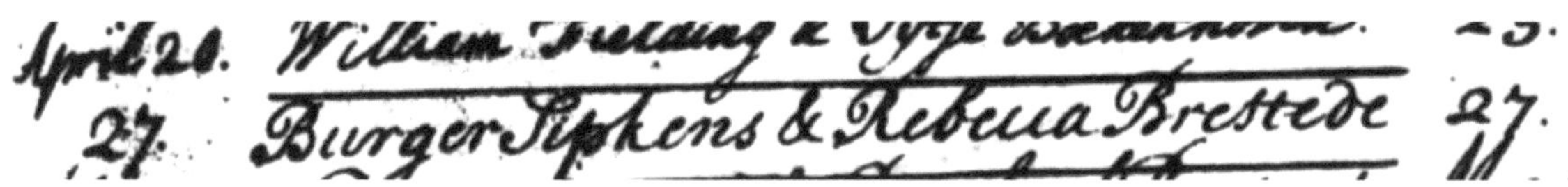

Husband:		Johannes Bresteede
	m:	Bef. 1713
	d:	Bet. 1722-1728
	Father:	
	Mother:	
	Other Spouses:	
Wife:		Rebecca Gerritse Onkelbach
	b:	08 Jan 1693 in New York
	d:	24 Aug 1755 in New York City, New York
	Father:	Gerrit Adamse Onkelbach
	Mother:	Elizabeth Van Schayck
	Other Spouses:	Burgher Sipkens
Children:		
1 F	Name:	Elizabeth Bresteede
	b:	07 Jan 1713 in New York City, New York
	Other Spouses:	
2 M	Name:	Andries Bresteede
	b:	20 Mar 1715 in New York City, New York
	Other Spouses:	
3 F	Name:	Annatje Bresteede
	b:	25 Jan 1716 in New York City, New York
	Other Spouses:	
4 M	Name:	Gerardus (Garrett) Bresteede
	b:	20 Aug 1718 in New York City, New York
	d:	Bef. 19 Mar 1747
	Other Spouses:	
5 F	Name:	Rebecca Bresteede
	b:	13 Jun 1722 in New York City, New York
	Other Spouses:	

Page 37.—In the name of God, Amen, July 10, 1732. I, GARRIT ONCKELBAG, of New York, distiller, being in health of body. My debts are to be paid. The rest of my estate, real and personal, I leave to my daughters, Nelly, wife of John Van Gelder, and Rebecca, wife of Burgher Sipkins, and to their heirs and assigns, and I make them and their husbands executors.

Witnesses, John Tilton, Walter Hyer, Hendricus Brevoort. Proved, May 21, 1733. At that time Burgher Sipkins was dead. His widow Rebecca was confirmed as one of the executors.

26

Children from wife #2:

1729 28 Sept; Burger Sipkens, Rebecca Onkelbag; **Burger**, 2 lingen, **Onkelbag**; Johannes Van Gelder, Elsje Sipkens, Gerrit Onkelbag, Elisabeth Brestede

Some time between the writing of his father-in-law's will dated July 10, 1732 and when it was proved on May 21, 1733, Burger Sipkens died. His widow Rebecca wrote her will in 1747.

Rebecca Sipkins Will

Abstracts of Wills Vol V 1754-1760, page 86:

Page 340.--In the name of God, Amen. I, REBECCA SIPKINS, of New York, widow, March 19, 1747. I leave to my grand child, Christina Breested, daughter of my late son, Garrett Breested, 100. I leave to my grand child, Cornelia Waldron, daughter of my late daughter, Elizabeth Griffith, deceased, 150. I leave to my three grand children, John, Rem, and Rebecca Remsen, children of my said daughter Elizabeth, deceased, each 50. To my grand child, Maria Vanderheuil, daughter of my late daughter, Johana Vanderheuil, 150. To my grand child, John Taylor, son of my daughter, Rebecca Griffith, 150. All these legacies are to be put at interest by my executors and the interest to be applied to their use for education and maintenance. I leave all the rest of my estate of every description to my daughter, Rebecca Griffith; and I make her and her husband, William Griffith, executors and guardians of my grand children.

Witnesses, William Bogert, Cornelius Boghart, Simon Johnson. Proved, December 5, 1755. Rebecca Griffith was then the surviving executor.

Endnotes

[1] Source: Amsterdam, Marriage proclamations by the churches, September 1653 – February 1654, DTB 472:255; consulted as "Ondertrouwregisters 1565-1811," index and digital images, Gemeente Amsterdam Stadsarchief (http://archief.amsterdam : accessed 5 July 2016).
[2] Yvette Hoitink. Dutch Genealogy Services Pelmolen 16 2406 KP Alphen aan den Rijn The Netherlands
[3] Source: Amsterdam, Marriage proclamations by the churches, May 1651 – May 1652, DTB 469:275; consulted as "Ondertrouwregisters 1565-1811," index and digital images, Gemeente Amsterdam Stadsarchief (http://archief.amsterdam : accessed 5 July 2016).
[4] Yvette Hoitink. Dutch Genealogy Services Pelmolen 16 2406 KP Alphen aan den Rijn The Netherlands
[5] Baptism Auckje - 30-10-1654 - Westerkerk - Hervormd - Aukes, Sepke - Jans, Baesje - DTB 105, p.19 – 000000054339
[6] 19-02-1683 - Cornelisz, Teunis - Sipkes, Aukje - DTB 511, p.77 - Huwelijksintekeningen van de KERK. - OTR00081000043
[7] DTB 77, p.446
[8] DTB 77, p.515
[9] DTB 77, p.577
[10] DTB 78, p.205
[11] Baptism of Jan - 20-09-1656 - Noorderkerk - Hervormd - Aukens, Zijppen - Jans, Baeffein - DTB 76, p.68 – 000000048129
[12] p. 329." Evjen, 419.
[13] Baptism , Evert - 27-08-1659 - Noorderkerk - Hervormd - Aukens, Sijppen - Jans, Barendje [sic] - DTB 76, p.170 - 000000048180
[14] Baptism Evert - 06-03-1661 - Noorderkerk - Hervormd - Aukeisz, Sepke - Jans, Baufein - DTB 76, p.216 – 000000048203
[15] Baptism , Vrouwtje - 14-10-1663 - Noorderkerk - Hervormd – Zwich [sic], Sipke - Jans, Baafje - DTB 76, p.291 – 000000048240
[16] 09-02-1697 - Ottes, Tjerck - Sipkes, Vroutje - DTB 527, p.17 - Huwelijksintekeningen van de KERK. - OTR00093000011
[17] Translation by Yvette Hoitink. Dutch Genealogy Services Pelmolen 16 2406 KP Alphen aan den Rijn The Netherlands
[18] Tierck - 13-12-1667 - Lutherse Kerk - Evangelisch-Luthers - Tiercks, Otte - Doedes, Maria - DTB 151, p.93 - 000000063660
[19] Ottesz, Tjerk - Sipkes, Vroutje - 02-09-1734 - Karthuizer Kerkhof - DTB 1176, p.24vo en p.25 - Weduwe van / Geb. - A04280000027
[20] Baptism Hendrick - 25-12-1665 - Noorderkerk - Hervormd - Auckes, Sipken - Jans, Baefje - DTB 76, p.362 – 000000048276
[21] Baptism , Evert - 02-10-1667 - Noorderkerk - Hervormd - Auckes, Sipken - Jans, Baefje - DTB 76, p.424 - 000000048307
[22] https://www.olivetreegenealogy.com/nn/church/rdcmarr1700.shtml
[23] http://www.olivetreegenealogy.com/nn/church/rdcmarr1702.shtml
[24] New York State Archives. New Netherland. Council. Dutch colonial council minutes, 1638-1665. Series A1809. Volume 8.

[25] 1669 29 Sep; Jan Janszen Poppen, jm van Amsterdam; Geertruydt Barents, wid Jan Hibon
[26] Collections of the New York Historical Society for the Year 1894

www.ingramcontent.com/pod-product-compliance
Lightning Source LLC
Chambersburg PA
CBHW040141240726
48664CB00002B/564